MACHINESE
WHISPERS

Illustrated by Steven Appleby

OLD STREET

*This volume is dedicated to
my imaginary friend George Mole,
without whom, hum, oh,
er, um, etc...*

First published October 2006
by Old Street Publishing Ltd

ISBN 1-905847-01-7   ISBN13 978-1-905847-01-3

Printed on paper made from trees grown from apple pips collected by small
children. Totally sustainable - so long as the children continue to collect
and plant the pips

Printed by WS Bookwell, Finland

Contents

*I*ntroduction

Machinese Whispers was first conceived as a humorous
refutation of the idea that computers can do anything
that humans can, only better. "My PC may be able to make
99,999,999,999,999 calculations every 1,000,000,000,000th
of a second," I reasoned, "but on the other hand it has
zero common sense or literary aptitude, and these absurd
mistranslations prove it."

For the most part, the book fulfils its original intention and
gives a much needed boost to human morale in the war of
advanced chip versus advanced chimp. In the language stakes
at least, computers show themselves to be laughably
unsophisticated, even deranged. The simplest phrases ("Do
not attempt this at home") are bafflingly altered ("Do not dry
this at home") and require an unusually advanced human, in
the form of Mr Appleby, to bring them to life.

Just occasionally, though, as if from a digital sage perched
on a lonely rock somewhere at the furthermost reaches of the
cyber universe, comes a whisper of true wisdom, truer and
more wise than the human version. The world would be a
more humane and a more humble place if we remembered
that all men are created not equal, but adequate. And,
perhaps, the same goes for computers.

Ben Yarde-Buller

I have nothing to declare
except my genie

Oscar Wilde

United we stand; divided we tumble

Aesop

United we stand; divided we fall

We hold these truths to be self-evident, that all men are created adequate

Thomas Jefferson

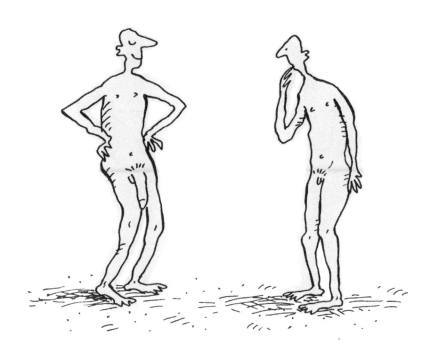

We hold these truths to be self-evident, that all men are created equal *Declaration of Independence*

Genius is one percent inhalation, ninety-nine percent sweat

Thomas Edison

Inspired by that sweating man I took a deep breath and invented this thing I call 'An Umbrella' – plus the 'Wellington Boot'.

Genius is one percent inspiration, ninety-nine percent perspiration

This Lady is not for rotation

Margaret Thatcher

This Lady is not for turning

The ballet or the bullet

Malcolm X

And 1964 looks like it might be the year
of the ballot or the bullet

The survival deconstruction is a question

Hamlet

To be or not to be: that is the question

Do not be afraid of largeness. Some are born large, some achieve largeness, and some have largeness pushed on top of them.

Twelfth Night

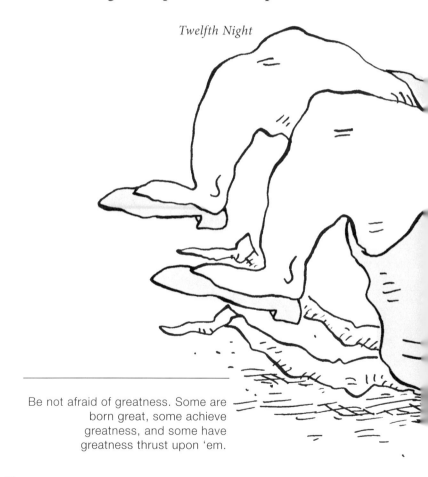

Be not afraid of greatness. Some are born great, some achieve greatness, and some have greatness thrust upon 'em.

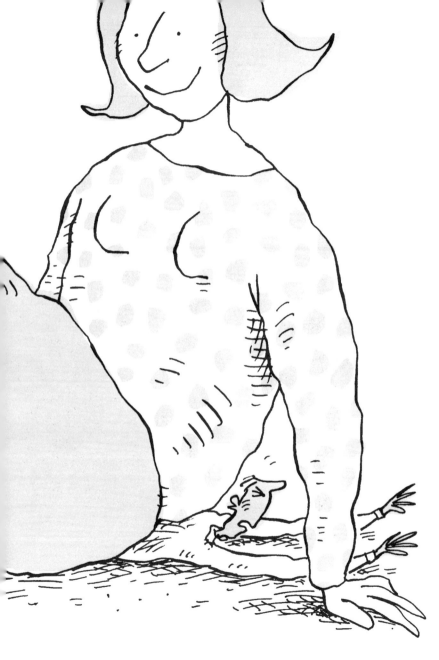

Here - look after your child

Rick Blaine, Casablanca

Here's looking at you, kid

The curse of true love never ran smooth

A Midsummer Night's Dream

The course of true love never did run smooth

I have always depended on the kindness of aliens

Blanche DuBois

I have always depended on the kindness of strangers
A Streetcar Named Desire

Friends, Romans, Countrymen:
Loan your ears to me!

Mark Antony

Friends, Romans, Countrymen: Lend me your ears!
Julius Caesar

What a piece of work is man! How aristocratic
in reason! How infinite in teachers
and administrators!

Hamlet

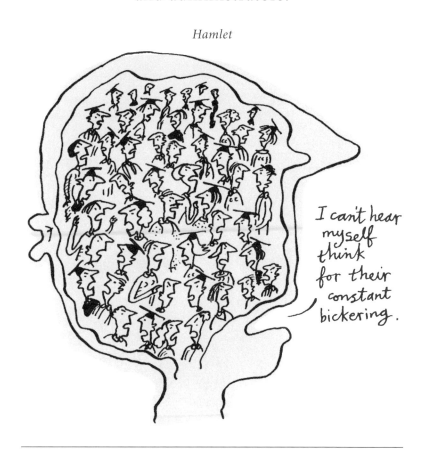

I can't hear
myself
think
for their
constant
bickering.

What a piece of work is a man! How noble in reason!
How infinite in faculty!

Part Three: **Miscellaneous**

Emergency!
The dog searches
carefully in the zone

Security! Dog patrols in the area

Do not dry this at home

Pay attention to the surface of the floor!

Caution! Slippery Floor Surface!

Your telephone is important to us.
Please do not make the telephone call.

Your call is important to us. Please do not hang up.

34

Excuse me, could I steal a light in addition to you?

Cigarettes cause your unborn child

Cigarettes damage the future of your child

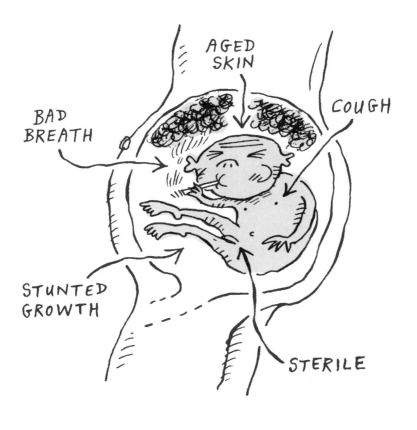

AGED SKIN

BAD BREATH

COUGH

STUNTED GROWTH

STERILE

Both: Cigarettes harm your unborn child

Stand Grandfather away from the closing doors

Stand clear of the closing doors

Twenty three pint luggers
and some itchy pigs, please

Coming up,
love.

Two pints of lager and some pork scatchings, please

Pleasant Time

1 - Gin hissing sound hissing sound sound

2 - American Liquor Sunrise

3 - Slaughtered on the Range

4 - Dust and Dirt

5 & 6 - Projectiles

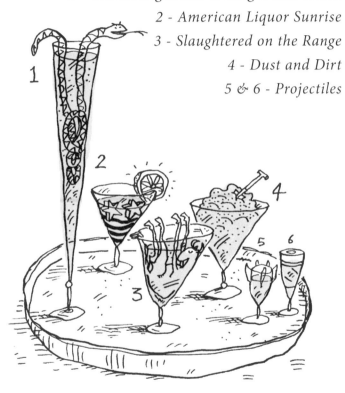

Happy Hour
1 - Gin Fizz 2 - Tequila Sunrise 3 - Sex on the Beach
4 - Gin and Tonic 5 & 6 - Shots

Menu
STARTERS: Vegetable Soup, Fish Soup MAIN COURSE: Steak and Chips DESSERTS: Baked Apple, Assorted Ice Creams

Keep up the step

Part Four: **Lyrics**

There's no business like the exposure business

Irving Berlin

There's no business like show business

Regulate Britannia!
Britannia regulates the waves!

James Thompson

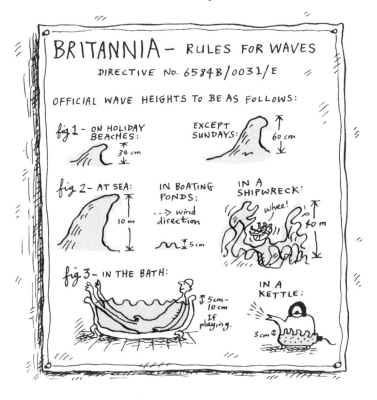

Cheers Miss American cake

Don Maclean

Bye Bye Miss American Pie

FLANGE OF THE JINGLE

OH, flange of the jingle, flange of the jingle
Jingle all the way
OH, what fun it is to be ridden,
By a horse in an open sleigh
Jingle the flange, flange of the jingle
Jingle all the way
OH, what fun it is to be ridden,
By a horse in an open sleigh

Oh, Jingle Bells, Jingle Bells, Jingle all the way!
Oh, what fun it is to ride in a one horse open sleigh!

On the Twelfth day of Christmas,
My true love sent to me:
Twelve beaters beating of the drum...

The Twelve Days of Christmas

On the twelfth day of Christmas, my true
love sent to me:
Twelve drummers drumming,
Eleven pipers piping,
Ten lords a-leaping,
Nine ladies dancing,
Eight maids a-milking,
Seven swans a-swimming,
Six geese a-laying,
Five golden rings,
Four calling birds,
Three French hens,
Two turtle doves,
And a partridge in a pear tree!

Eleven pipers that install tubes...

Ten Your Excellency leaps...

Nine injuries dancing...

Eight servants' milk...

Seven swans a floating...

Six inserting geese...

59

Five golden yellow rings...

Four appealing birds...

Three French chickens...

Two tortoise studs...

And a partridge
in a tree of pear-trees!

I strolled the lonely achievement cloud
That float in high o'er valley and hill
When at the same time me saw the crowd,
Many golden yellow narcissuses
Nearby lake, under tree
Inspires the wing and dances in the breeze

William Wordsworth

I wandered lonely as a cloud / That floats on high o'er
vales and hills / When all at once I saw a crowd / A host, of
golden daffodils / Beside the lake, beneath the trees /
Fluttering and dancing in the breeze

They have sexual intercourse,
your mother and father
They may not mean to, but they do

Philip Larkin

They fuck you up, your Mum and Dad
They may not mean to, but they do

Do I have to compare thee with a summer's day?

William Shakespeare

Shall I compare thee to a summer's day?

Lolita, light of my life, fire of my lumbar regions

Vladimir Nabokov

Lolita, light of my life, fire of my loins

That before us the time was best before us,
that time it was worst, the light which is
incredulity and that new era which are
conviction and that new era which are
foolishness and that age which are intelligence
and that age which that are, the darkness which
is that season, the winter of the despair which is
desire and that spring which are that season, us
what which us it did not have everything which
it had, entirely was we who go to the heaven
which is we directly, the other method of going
and indicating entirely - in other words,
there was a period...

Charles Dickens

It was the best of times, it was the worst of times, it was
the age of wisdom, it was the age of foolishness, it was the
epoch of belief, it was the epoch of incredulity, it was the
season of Light, it was the season of Darkness, it was the
spring of hope, it was the winter of despair, we had everything before us, we had nothing before us, we were all going
direct to Heaven, we were all going direct the other way - in
short, the period was so far like the present period...
A Tale of Two Cities

73

Emma Woodhouse, nice, nice, and rich, with a convenient home and a happy disposal, seemed to unite some of best blessings of existence

Jane Austen

A happy disposal is all very well but 'NICE' TWICE implies BLAND and FAT and UGLY with low self-esteem!

Emma Woodhouse, handsome, clever, and rich, with a comfortable home and happy disposition, seemed to unite some of the best blessings of existence *Emma*

To His Bashful Housewife

Andrew Marvell

Abandon hope all ye who enter here! *Inferno*

In the Beginning
the God created the sky
and the ground

The Bible

In the beginning God created the heaven and the earth

CLICK!

And the God said,
Let there be light:
and there was,
slightly

The Bible

And God said, Let there be light:
and there was light

Jerusalem

William Blake

And did that old foot in ancient time
Pace on the green hillocks of United Kingdom?
And is god's saintly lamb
Seen in God's pleasant pasture of United Kingdom?

And did the face of the priest
Glare on our cloudy hillocks?
And did he construct Jerusalem
Among these dark devil mills?

Bring me my bow-tie of very hot gold!
Bring me my arrows of craving!
Bring me my bud! O the clouds explain!
Bring me my two-wheeled tank of fire!

I will not cease from intellectual combat,
Nor will me sword sleep in me hand
Until we have built Jerusalem
On the green ground and joke of England.

Jerusalem
And did those feet in ancient time / Walk upon England's mountains
green? / And was the holy Lamb of God / On England's pleasant
pastures seen? / And did the Countenance Divine / Shine forth
upon our clouded hills? / And was Jerusalem builded here / Among
these dark Satanic Mills? / Bring me my Bow of burning gold: /
Bring me my Arrows of desire: / Bring me my Spear: O clouds
unfold! / Bring me my Chariot of fire. / I shall not cease from Mental
Fight / Nor shall my Sword sleep in my hand / Till we have built
Jerusalem / In England's green & pleasant Land.

Coo...

False witness of bear shalt thou not against thy neighbour

The Bible

Thou shalt not bear false witness against thy neighbour

THE ATTENTION ATTEMPT

Our Father,
He who art in sky,
The respect is thy name

The Lord's Prayer
Our Father / Who art in Heaven / Hallowed be thy name

Afterlife Thy

Thy will be fact,
On earth
as it is in the sky

Can I touch
you? Just to
prove to myself
that you
exist...

If you do I'll
smite you with
a thunderbolt.

Thy will be done / On earth as it is in Heaven

Whoops...

Give to us this day our bread vital

And forgive us our penetrations

Since we forgive those that
tramble adversely on us.

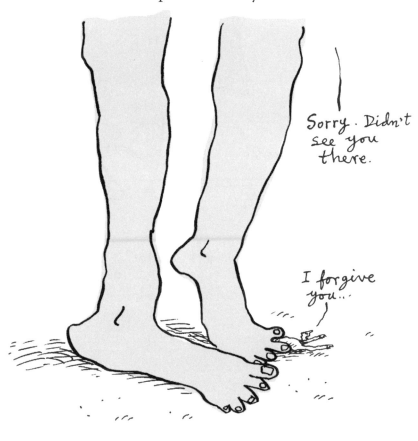

As we forgive those who trespass against us

Do not lead us in seduction,
But give birth to us from badness.

Lead us not into temptation / But deliver us from evil

For Thine is the kingdom,
And the Energy and the Fame

For Thine is the kingdom / The Power and the Glory

For Always and Always

Love